Contents

1   The history of sport 4

2   The media 12

3   Amateurs and professionals 20

4   Drugs and sport 24

5   Politics and sport 36

6   Technological change and sport 41

    Glossary 46

    Find out more 47

    Index 48

Any words appearing in the text in bold, **like this**, are explained in the glossary.

The history of sport

Origins

As they become increasingly health-conscious, more and more people are taking up sports and physical activities as an enjoyable way of spending their leisure time. Sport is seen as very important, not only by sportspeople but also by many other people who enjoy doing something that improves health, as well as bringing many hidden benefits. Sport has an impact on many areas of society, but how did it all start?

Many of the techniques used in sport today had their origins in hunting, fighting and the general survival skills needed by our distant ancestors. In primitive cultures and early civilizations the fittest survived. Those who could throw spears accurately and powerfully, who could track, chase and catch food, and who were strong enough to fight against enemies were the ones who lived longest.

During those times there were no countries or nations as we know them today, but people lived in groups as communities. From this, small settlements developed, then towns and cities, and eventually nations. As time went by, people saw the need to protect the communities they lived in. Gradually this led to the formation of armies. The regular training of soldiers led in turn to the development of many sporting activities, especially combat sports.

Armies needed to be ready for battle. They also needed to be kept occupied and fit, and they achieved this through practice and training. Much of this involved an element of competition. Wrestling and boxing developed from these activities (the Olympic wrestling event is still known as Greco Roman wrestling) and many of the **martial arts** that are popular today also began at this time, in the East.

The first stadiums designed to stage these sports were built by the Romans. The events often involved men fighting against each other, and against animals.

It is interesting to note that the shape of these stadiums has not changed very much since Roman times, although now the facilities are likely to be very different.

Much of the sport that went on in the Roman amphitheatres was very cruel and violent. It often involved animals or men fighting against each other to the death.

Sporting contests evolved over the years and became more related to skill, strength and stamina. One of the first recorded gymnastic-type activities occurred 3,000 years ago in Crete (in the Minoan period) when young men and women used to perform bull dances. They would vault over the head of a bull, using the horns to grip on

Amphitheatres

Five thousand animals are recorded as being killed in one day in AD 80, in one amphitheatre. There is also a record of 400 bears and 300 lions being killed in one day during the reign of the emperor Nero.

Aspects of P.E.

Sport in Society

Kirk Bizley

www.heinemann.co.uk/library
Visit our website to find out more information about Heinemann Library books.

To order:
 Phone ++44 (0) 1865 888066
 Send a fax to ++44 (0) 1865 314091
Visit the Heinemann Bookshop at www.heinemann.co.uk/library to browse our catalogue and order online.

First published in Great Britain by Heinemann Library, Halley Court, Jordan Hill, Oxford OX2 8EJ, part of Harcourt Education. Heinemann is a registered trademark of Harcourt Education Ltd.

© Harcourt Education Ltd 1999, 2007
2nd edition first published in paperback in 2008.
The moral right of the proprietor has been asserted.

Editorial: Andrew Farrow
Design: Joanna Hinton-Malivoire
Picture research: Hannah Taylor
Production: Duncan Gilbert

Originated by Dot Gradations Ltd
Printed and bound in China by CTPS

ISBN 978 0 4310 7879 3 (hardback)
11 10 09 08 07
10 9 8 7 6 5 4 3 2 1

ISBN 978 0 4310 7886 1 (paperback)
12 11 10 09 08
10 9 8 7 6 5 4 3 2 1

British Library Cataloguing in Publication Data
Bizley, Kirk
Sport in society. – 2nd ed. - (Aspects of P.E.)
306.4'83
A full catalogue record for this book is available from the British Library.

Acknowledgements
The publishers would like to thank the following for permission to reproduce photographs:
Action Plus pp. **15** (Glyn Kirk), **30**, **36** (Neil Tingle), **43** (Glyn Kirk), **45** (Richard Francis); Allsport p. **18**; ASP (George Herringshaw) p. **28**; Associated Press p. **37**; Barnaby's Picture Library p. **38**; Coloursport (Andrew Cowie) p. **40**; Corbis p. **16** (EPA/Dominic Ebenbichler); Empics (Neil Simpson) p. **42**; Getty Images pp. **12** (AFP/Adrian Dennis), **19** (Christopher Furlong), **34** (Julian Finney), **41 (left)** (Julian Finney); Hulton Deutsch pp. **7**, **21**, **22**; Hulton Getty p. **6**; Image Bank p. **24**; Michael Cole pp. **41 (right)**, **44**; Mike Brett Photography p. **23**; Rex Features p. **18**; Robert Harding Picture Library pp. **5** (A. Tovy), **13**; Science Photo Library (Krassovsky) p. **26**; Trinity Newspapers p. **20**.

Cover photograph of Christiano Ronaldo and Ryan Giggs reproduced with permission of Getty Images (AFP/Adrian Dennis).

The author and publishers would like to thank Nuala Mullan and Doug Neate for their comments in the preparation of the first edition of this book.

Disclaimer
All the Internet addresses (URLs) given in this book were valid at the time of going to press. However, due to the dynamic nature of the Internet, some addresses may have changed, or sites may have changed or ceased to exist since publication. While the author and publishers regret any inconvenience this may cause readers, no responsibility for any such changes can be accepted by either the author or the publishers.

To the memory of my dear father

The Colosseum in Rome is where the ancient Romans held brutal competitions.

to the animal's back and then somersault off on to the ground behind them. This was almost certainly performed in front of spectators, and was an important ceremony.

Horses were also linked with sport very early on. As long ago as 1350 BC, horses were trained and used for war and combat, so it was essential to be able to ride well. From this, and chariot racing, the sports of horse racing and showjumping have evolved.

Contests between men also started many years ago. There are drawings on the walls of Egyptian tombs dating from 2300 BC that clearly show some wrestling techniques. Modern Olympic wrestling is very similar to that of more than 4,000 years ago.

There is no doubt that sport in some form has existed in all cultures throughout the world for thousands of years. Cave paintings that are 20,000 years old showing hunters with basic weapons, also clearly show the movements made.

Judo

One of the most popular martial arts is judo, which dates in its present form from the late 15th century – not as ancient as is generally believed. However, it probably had its roots in the activities of the samurai warriors in Japan.

The marathon winner in the 1908 Olympic Games crosses the line.

Sport gets organized

Considering sporting contests and activities have been taking place for centuries, organized sport has developed relatively recently. It has its roots in the various types of combat, competition and festivals that went before.

The ancient Greek Olympics are probably the best-known and earliest example of organized sports. Several thousand years ago, the many states that made up Greece were almost constantly at war with each other. However, they would stop fighting at intervals to have a contest of athletics, wrestling and combat between contestants from the various states. This competition was held at the temple of Zeus, at Olympia. The first recorded contest took place in 776 BC and lasted for seven days.

The Olympian Games, as they were known, were one of four ancient games held by the Greeks.

The other Greek games were the Isthmian, Pythian and Nemean games. It was the Olympian games that generated the most interest, though. Envoys would be sent out early in the year to get all of the contestants ready. There were even facilities made available for some of the contestants to prepare and train before the games. There was a ruling that the competitors had to train for a month before the start of the games, and the whole event was treated very seriously. The winner of each event would receive an olive wreath as a prize. These winners were then looked after by their home cities, living lives of comparative luxury at public expense!

The ancient Romans also had a form of games dedicated to their gods, and these involved more brutal types of competition including fights to the death.

The Greeks were responsible for the start of one very famous contest – the marathon.

In 490 BC the ancient Greek army defeated the Persians at a place called Marathon and a runner, called Pheidippides, ran from Marathon to Athens with the news. History says he collapsed and died of exhaustion just after he arrived. The marathon distance is now set at 42.195 km (26 miles 385 yards) because that is the distance over which the 1908 Olympic race was run. The actual distance from Marathon to Athens was about 35 km (22 miles) and later races were run over about 42 km (26 miles). The 1908 games required the runners to run an extra 195 metres so that they could finish opposite the Royal Box at the White City stadium. This has been the standard distance ever since.

Sporting contests have been held all over the world. There were many local customs associated with the events, some of which still take place today.

A form of football is recorded as being played as long ago as AD 1352. Villages competed against each other, and the aim was to get a ball from one village to the next. There were no particular rules and the 'game' was often so rough that it was not unheard of for people to be killed.

Various games played with balls, and with bats and balls, were played all over the world and parts of some games were copied, or adapted, to invent other games. The main reason that these games tended to be based locally was because there was no transport. It was not possible to play against anyone except neighbouring teams. It was quite unusual – and took a long time – for anyone to travel from one country to another. The people who went on the very first cricket tours overseas travelled by ship. The journey to the host country could take several weeks, before any of the cricket matches even started.

As transport started to improve and sport became better organized, competitions between areas within countries, and between different countries, could take place.

Chariot racing was an exciting and dangerous event at ancient Roman games.

Due to improved transportation, national and international sport became possible. This led to a need for the rules and regulations to be agreed and written down. This, in turn, has led to national and international bodies being formed to regulate the huge amount of international sport that is played today.

All of the sports, and the major sporting competitions, have governing bodies with overall responsibility for their own particular sports. This has not always been a trouble-free system and some sports have rather a large number of organizations claiming to be in charge internationally. Boxing is perhaps the best example of this: there are now four different organizations that claim to have jurisdiction over the sport and they all have their own world championships. There seems to be enough interest and money in the sport to support all of these bodies, which shows how much sport has evolved over a comparatively short space of time.

How sports evolved

The development and histories of some of today's most popular sports are fascinating.

Athletics

Athletics involves track and field events, which have their origins in the Greek games of more than 4,000 years ago. Field events include the high jump, long jump, pole vault and triple jump, as well as throwing events such as the discus, javelin, shot-put and hammer. Track events include all of the running events.

Many of the field events are clearly based on hunting skills and the track events are straightforward tests of strength, speed, skill and stamina. All of them are tests of power. It is easy to see how athletics has developed and remained popular over the centuries.

Basketball

Basketball was invented in the United States in 1891 by Dr James Naismith, a professor of physical education at the University of Kansas. The game was originally played using peach baskets (which gave the sport its name) nailed to the walls at each end of the gymnasium.

It is very unusual to be able to trace the origin of a game as accurately as we can for basketball. It is even possible to state the day on which the first game was ever played – 20 January 1892!

Netball

The game of netball was originally played as a version of basketball. It started in England in 1895 when a visiting American, Dr Toles, introduced basketball. The game was gradually modified to make it better suited to women, and netball emerged. Today, netball is mainly played outdoors, by women, while basketball is mainly played indoors, by men.

Baseball

Some people claim that baseball is a version of rounders, which was introduced into North America in the 18th century by the early settlers. Settlers from Europe arrived in North America in the 17th century and there is a very strong likelihood that they were the originators of the game.

Some people believe that baseball evolved from a variety of different games originating from stick and ball games that have been played since the early days of civilization. There is evidence of these types of games being played in the ancient cultures of Greece, Persia and Egypt, and they became popular in Europe during the Middle Ages.

Many Americans, though, claim that the game was invented by Abner Doubleday in Cooperstown, New York in 1839. This is why the United States' Baseball Hall of Fame is based there.

Cricket

Cricket bats have been found that date as far back as 1750. In 1774 the game was played with two stumps with a single bail between them. The third stump was added in 1776.

Records seem to show that cricket has existed in some form since the 13th century. Thomas Lord founded the Marylebone Cricket Club (**MCC**) in 1787 and the Lords cricket ground is named after him. Originally, underarm bowling was used, but in 1864 full overarm bowling was allowed. Many other changes have been allowed since, but all have to be agreed by the MCC, which still sets all the rules of the game.

Cricket is one of the oldest international games. The first **test match** (international event) was played between England and Australia in 1877, and an English side toured in Australia as early as 1861.

The introduction of the one-day game format into cricket, where there is a limited number of overs for each team and a match is decided in one day, has given the game a big boost internationally and made it more interesting for many of the spectators.

In many countries the one-day games subsidize the more traditional five-day test matches as they are far more popular with the fans.

Hat tricks

Cricket is responsible for a famous sporting term. In the early days of the game a bowler would be given a top hat if he took three wickets in succession. This was the origin of the term **hat trick**.

W. G. Grace, born in 1848, was England's best cricketer of the time.

Football

The ancient Chinese played what could be called a version of football, kicking the severed head of a defeated enemy around the battle area! From these gruesome beginnings, football has evolved to its present form and has become one of the most popular sports in the world.

The Football Association (**FA**) was formed in England in 1863, when it started to work out the agreed rules. Before long there was an organized administrative structure to run the game. The first international match took place between England and Scotland in 1872. The result was a goalless draw.

Professional football was allowed from 1885, which makes it one of the oldest professional sports in existence. The first FA Cup competition was held in 1871 and there were 15 entries. The growth of the professional game led to football stadiums being built in many of the major cities in the UK. Most of the cities soon had at least one professional team and some (such as London) had more.

The **World Cup** was first organized in 1930 and was played in Uruguay. The host country went on to win the Cup.

The World Cup is now one of the major international sporting events. It was estimated that over 280 milli≠on television viewers watched the 2006 World Cup final, which was played in Germany. The international organization that runs football, **FIFA**, has more than 160 nations affiliated to it and also runs the International Board, which considers and announces any rule changes that they think appropriate.

Rugby

In 1823, William Webb Ellis, a pupil at Rugby school in England, picked up a football during a game and ran with it. He is credited with starting the game of rugby football. The game took its name from the school where it was first played.

In 1895 there was an argument over whether players should be allowed to be paid to play rugby. This caused a split in the game. Rugby Union (played with 15 players on each side) was the **amateur** version of the game and Rugby League (with 13 players on each side) was the professional version. The two games are quite similar, although they are played to different rules. This rift between the two forms of the game lasted for 100 years, but in 1995, they sorted out their differences and Rugby Union players were allowed openly to earn money from the game. Up until then, there were very strict rules enforced by the Rugby Union ruling bodies – anyone who played Rugby League was banned for life from playing (or even being connected with) Rugby Union.

Rugby Union took longer than football to stage its own World Cup, which was held in 1987 and was won by New Zealand. The cup is called the William Webb Ellis Trophy, after the originator of the game, an≠d is competed for every four years.

Tennis

Real tennis was played in the Middle Ages and **lawn tennis** (originally called 'tennis-on-the-lawn') started in the 19th century. Major Walter Clopton Wingfield, a British army officer, has been credited with inventing the game. There are also claims that it is based on an ancient Greek game called **sphairistike**, as were badminton and squash.

The first international tennis championships for men were held in 1877, at the All England Lawn Tennis and Croquet Club in Wimbledon. The Wimbledon Championship is still recognized as the major championship today. In 1884 women were included as well.

There seems to be a very close link between tennis and squash. In the 18th century, inmates at Fleet prison used to hit a ball against the prison wall. In 1850, pupils at Harrow school used to practise against a wall while they waited to play 'rackets' in an indoor court. They used a slow, squashy ball – and so the game of squash started to evolve.

Table tennis started as a game played between two students at Cambridge University. They used two cigar boxes as bats and a champagne cork as a ball!

Hockey

There is evidence of hockey being played as long ago as 3 BC. The ancient Greeks, Egyptians and Romans played a version of hockey. The games of **hurling** and **shinty**, both played in Ireland, are variations of hockey.

American football

American football developed in the United States in the 19th century, and was based on football and rugby. The ancient Greeks had a similar game that was called **harpaston**, also based on getting a ball across a line, but in their version there was no limit to the number of players allowed on each team.

The first professional game of American Football was played in 1895 in Latrobe, Pennsylvania, but it was slow to take off as a major attraction. It was not until 1920 that the American Professional Football Association was formed, then the National Football League (**NFL**) was formed in 1922. The NFL is now one of the most powerful sporting bodies in the world. It controls the game in the United States and has been promoting it and establishing it internationally. The vital, final match called the **Super Bowl** is the climax of the season and it has the biggest television audience of any of the major events.

Super Bowl

Of the ten most watched television programmes ever, the Super Bowl features seven times.

In the United States, 'Super Bowl Sunday' is a tradition in many households. The main event is accompanied by performances from top music stars. Janet Jackson, Justin Timberlake, The Rolling Stones and Prince are just a few of the musicians who have appeared. The Super Bowl is also broadcast live around the world – including to the UK. Fans of American football have to stay up late to catch the live action though!

2) The media

The media, consisting of television, radio, newspapers, magazines, books and the Internet, have enormous influence on modern sport. In fact, the wide choice offered by satellite and cable television has only been available in the last 20 years and the growth of the Internet has been even more recent.

Television

Television is arguably the most powerful of all forms of the media, especially since linked satellite networks have enabled programmes to be beamed live around the world. In the UK, sport on television has been regulated and controlled since the Television Act of 1954 – which shows how recent the growth of television has been. This Act gave the Government powers to draw up a list of protected events, known as **listed events**. These cannot be shown exclusively on **pay per view** channels (cable or satellite channels where the viewer has to pay extra for the service). These listed events are shown on **terrestrial television** (TV stations that can be received in all homes using an aerial or digital receiver). These lists have been amended over the years. The last major change, in 1996–97, resulted in:

Group A (Full Live Coverage Protected)

- The Olympic Games
- The **FIFA World Cup** finals tournament
- The European Football Championship finals tournament
- The **FA** Cup final
- The Scottish FA Cup final (in Scotland)
- The Grand National
- The Derby
- The Wimbledon tennis finals
- The Rugby League Challenge Cup final
- The Rugby World Cup final

Group B (Secondary Coverage Protected)

- Cricket **test matches** played in England
- Non-finals play in the Wimbledon tournament
- All other matches in the Rugby World Cup finals tournament

Many sports events have some form of TV coverage. Modern technology and the demands of the viewing public mean that coverage is often close-up and replayed from many angles. Here, England goalkeeper Paul Robinson is being filmed at a 2006 World Cup match against Paraguay.

- Six Nations Rugby tournament matches involving home countries

- The Commonwealth Games

- The World Athletics Championship

- The Cricket World Cup – the final, semi-finals and matches involving home nations' teams

- The Ryder Cup

- The Open Golf Championship

These events are 'listed' to make sure that everyone who wants to watch what are regarded as the nation's major sporting events can do so. For the category B events, satellite providers can provide live coverage as long as adequate arrangements are made for delayed coverage or highlights on BBC1, BBC2, ITV1 (Channel 3) or Channel 4.

Terrestrial television

In the UK there are five television stations (BBC 1, BBC 2, ITV, Channel 4 and Channel 5) that can be broadcast to every home. For many people, these are the only stations on which they can watch televised sport.

Television coverage of sport has been popular ever since transmissions first started in 1936. (The BBC had started in 1922 but it only broadcast on the radio.) Live coverage of sporting events soon became very popular, although many technological advances in cameras and transmitters were needed before all of this became possible.

Satellite and cable services

Sky launched its first Sky Sports channel on the Astra satellite in 1991 and it became available, by subscription, in 1992. In August 1994, a second Sky Sports channel was launched and in 1996 a third was added. Since then, Sky has added a further five sports channels. Along with Eurosport channels, and many more, satellite subscribers now have a huge range of sports channels to choose from – 24 hours a day.

It is a measure of its popularity that there are more stations dedicated to sport than to any other subject. There is also a lot of financial interest in sport.

In 1992, Sky obtained the rights to show live Premier League football, with a successful bid of £304 million. For this sum, it was allowed to transmit the games live on the various Sky Sports channels. Either the BBC or ITV was then allowed to show recorded highlights later. However, following a lengthy legal battle with the European Commission, which deemed the exclusivity of these rights to be against the interests of competition and the consumer, BSkyB's **monopoly** will come to an end from the beginning of the 2007–08 season. In May 2006 the Irish broadcaster Setanta Sports was awarded two of the six Premiership packages that the English FA offered to broadcasters. Sky picked up the remaining four for a staggering £1.3 billion!

The cable and satellite companies rely heavily on sport because it makes up about half of their programme output. With the advent of interactive services they are also able to increase coverage even further by allowing more options within each channel. This means viewers can watch a wide variety of different matches or games. The satellite companies are able to devote a whole channel to sport, without transmitting other features. This is an advantage because they can show uninterrupted coverage of events, no matter how long they last.

There has also been a growth in pay per view events where subscribers pay extra for special sporting events such as boxing contests or additional football matches. Several major football clubs, such as Manchester United and Chelsea, have also launched their own dedicated channels to cover all of their own matches.

Television and sponsorship

The relationship between the TV companies and sponsors is very complex and controversial. In 1994, a government committee recommended that the BBC should stop broadcasting any sporting events sponsored by tobacco companies. The ITV network had already stopped this in 1987 and had its own Code of Programme Sponsorship, which clearly laid out what is, and what is not, acceptable sponsorship. Tobacco sponsorship of sports finally ended in 2003.

Sponsorship was obviously identified as a sensitive area because all the guidelines have been very clearly set out. No news or current affairs programme may be sponsored but all – or part – of other programmes can be, provided general guidelines are followed. The main rules are that the sponsors must:

• not be allowed any undue influence

• be clearly identified at the beginning and end of the programme

• be manufacturers or suppliers of acceptable products.

Sponsors themselves like the coverage because it is a form of advertising for them, and they can be assured of large audiences. Some of the highest viewing figures for any programmes in any year are for sporting events. Sports sponsors can gain the additional benefit of being associated with something that has a good, healthy image.

Types of programme

The many different ways in which television both shows and promotes sport include:

• live sporting action

• highlights programmes

• documentaries

• quiz programmes

• news bulletins

• information services (such as BBC interactive, **Ceefax** and **teletext**)

• coverage of major sporting events

• drama series

• sporting 'magazine' programmes.

Tobacco sponsorship

For any one of the televised Formula One Grand Prix races, the organizers can expect a worldwide audience of about 400 million. Following the final banning of tobacco company and brand names on cars, the companies tried to get around the regulation by using logos or colour schemes similar to their usual adverts to promote their products at races. The 2006 Snooker World Championship was the first one in 30 years not to be sponsored by Embassy cigarettes!

One of the main reasons for the large and varied amount of sporting coverage is that sport is relatively cheap to televise. Many other programmes are far more expensive to produce and they do not have the uncertainty and drama that a live sports event can bring. It is clear that televised sport is very popular, with huge audience demand.

Benefits television brings to sport

Television clearly benefits from showing sport, but it does work both ways. Sport benefits through:

• *increased popularity* – many minority sports have increased in popularity, and boosted their numbers of participants, through TV coverage. For example, gymnastics nearly always has a boom period immediately following an Olympic Games when there is extensive coverage.

• *increased revenue* – income from sponsorship and endorsement of products can go directly to the sports or clubs

• *direct payments* – television has to pay for the rights to broadcast events and this is often one of the main sources of income for some of the governing bodies and their clubs.

TV quiz programmes, such as *A Question of Sport*, combine sporting facts and clips with fun, to appeal to a wider audience. Even non-sports-fans can watch and enjoy these programmes and perhaps be encouraged to take a greater interest in sport.

Conflicts between television and sport

Most of the time TV brings great benefits to sport, but there are some occasions when there are problems.

- Television may intrude upon an event – cameras, cables, commentators' positions, lighting and sound crews can all get in the way of the spectators who have paid to come and watch. The TV companies want the best views for their audiences but this could inconvenience the paying spectators.

- Timings can be dictated by the TV companies and the audience may have to wait until the broadcast is ready to start. On some occasions the entire starting time of the event is decided by the TV companies. For an international event the timing is often scheduled for the largest audience in one particular country – frequently the United States. This would mean a start in the early hours of the morning in Europe, to satisfy US viewers.

- The use of replays, both in slow motion and from various angles, can undermine the authority of officials, who do not have the benefit of these facilities. Many panellists and commentators can sit in judgement of decisions. The TV companies demand that they can see all of the action from every angle and they have the technology to repeat the action very quickly – sometimes even on screens at the grounds.

- If particular sports are not covered on TV they may decline in popularity and participation in them may drop off. Television tends to concentrate on the major sports that attract the largest audiences, because this is what the sponsors and the advertisers want. Many games such as hockey and netball do not attract the same degree of TV coverage that football, rugby and cricket receive.

- If a match or activity is shown live on TV, fewer spectators may actually go along to watch the live event. This leads to a drop in revenue for clubs, which rely on the money they take from spectators. Therefore, many sports organizations have arrangements to set aside some money that can be shared among all of the clubs, at the end of

The use of new technology can increase the enjoyment for spectators, but also put players and officials under increased pressure to get things right. In some tennis matches, players can have decisions reviewed on a replay screen, such as this one in Miami, Florida, USA.

the season, so that they do not make financial losses.

- Televising one event live may encourage people to stay at home to watch, and not attend another sporting event or fixture. This means that a totally different sport could suffer!

Despite all these factors, however, the benefits of televising sport do appear to outweigh the disadvantages – otherwise it is unlikely that there would be so much sports coverage on television.

Technological developments are being made all the time, and television is constantly looking at ways of improving sports coverage. These include:

- small cameras being placed in the stumps to obtain close shots in cricket

- Formula One racing cars carrying cameras in their bodywork

- officials using radio links to the TV directors and commentators, who can hear why certain decisions are made.

Far more cameras – many remotely controlled – are used to cover all aspects of the game. Following the introduction of interactive services it is now possible for viewers to choose which TV camera coverage they view, camera angles, and even specific players or officials to watch.

Radio

Most radio stations cover sport in much the same format as television. One of the main advantages radio has over TV is the large number of local stations that can cover local sport and teams. They do not have to rely on the big sporting events to attract listeners, as they can concentrate on any sport that is of local importance.

Obviously the radio stations don't broadcast pictures. Therefore they are not considered as rivals by the TV companies, and in particular the satellite companies. This means that they normally cover all of the major sporting events. Even the pay per view events on TV are usually covered live by the radio stations. In fact, they can even cover live events that none of the TV companies are allowed to broadcast! The introduction of DAB digital radio has made it possible for many more specialist sports radio stations to operate, including BBC Five Live Sports Extra, which commenced broadcasting in February 2002.

Some specialist radio stations concentrate largely or solely on sports coverage. Radio Five Live in the UK is a good example of this. It concentrates on news and sport, and its large output of live coverage includes sporting events, such as athletics and major championships, as well as boxing, football and cricket. The specialist radio stations can use satellite link-ups to cover sport from all over the world, and use the telephone networks to get the information broadcast.

The overall advantages that radio has over television include:

- broadcasting costs are much lower as only one commentator is needed (although sometimes they also have an expert analyst to add some comments), and the technology required to transmit the broadcast can be more basic than for TV.

- radios are very cheap, they are portable and listeners can tune in when they are gardening or driving in their cars, so the potential audience is very large.

The way the press covers sports events can change the way the public supports players and teams. In 2006, newspapers were very critical of the decision to allow the wives, girlfriends and children of players to be with the England football team during the World Cup. Here, Brooklyn Beckham, Cheryl Tweedy and Victoria Beckham are watching England play Portugal.

The press

The press includes newspapers, magazines books and the Internet. All of these can be very influential and cover sport and sporting issues in a variety of ways.

Newspapers

All daily newspapers have sports sections, usually at the back, and some of them even have extra supplements for all the sporting news and results. Major sport often occurs at the weekends, when most people are free to watch sporting events. The Sunday papers, therefore, usually offer very extensive sports coverage.

Press conferences are very common, where the press (and other areas of the media) have the opportunity to interview sporting personalities. This includes not only the players themselves but also the managers and coaches. Many sports organizations insist that these press conferences take place. The press have the right to ask whoever they want to attend. Failure to do so can result in a fine or even a ban.

In many of the major US sports the players have a clause in their contracts that makes them available for interviews whenever requested. **Locker room interviews** (interviews with the players in the changing rooms immediately after the game) are very common as a result of this.

Newspapers are very influential because they publish the results, match reports, team news, rule changes and fixtures. They also comment on many major sporting issues and personalities.

After a series of poor results in the early 1990s, many newspapers were very critical of the then England football manager, Graham Taylor. There was a campaign to get him sacked, which was eventually successful in 1993. There is little doubt that the extensive press coverage influenced this. Similarly, newspaper revelations about the private life and professional behaviour of Sven-Goran Eriksson led him to give up the manager's job in 2006.

Magazines

The number of specialist sporting magazines has increased rapidly in recent years. Most sports have at least one publication devoted to them. These magazines concentrate on issues to do with their sports, often printing very detailed information of interest to keen fans. Some of the major clubs even have their own fan magazines published. These are sold throughout the country, not just in the area where the team is based.

General sporting magazines are also proving popular and these look at all of the current issues in sport today. These magazines are usually printed monthly, but there are some that come out weekly.

Books

Books related to sport fall into a number of categories, from novels to textbooks that deal with particular aspects of sport. Some of the most controversial books of recent years have been **autobiographies** by famous sportspeople that have referred to incidents in their careers.

Many sports personalities write books about their lives. Manchester United and England footballer Wayne Rooney launched the first part of his autobiography in 2006, when he was only 20 years old.

For many sporting personalities, writing a book is a way of earning extra money once their playing careers are at an end. It is also a way for **amateurs** to earn money without being thought of as **professional** performers.

Many other sporting personalities make a living from being **journalists** and writing for newspapers, as well as appearing on television – commenting on the sport they have taken part in.

Internet

The Internet has only been widely available since the mid-1990s. The very rapid growth of computer technology, ICT developments, and widespread access in homes and businesses has meant that this is now the fastest growing area of the media. Users can access information and visual images, chat with other people online, and watch live performances. Increasingly, new technology is allowing Internet access to sport across platforms such as mobile phones and home media centres.

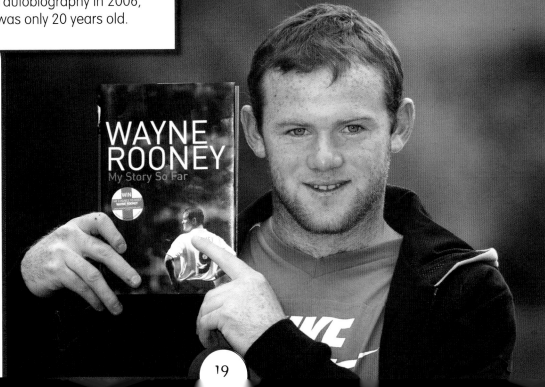

3) Amateurs and professionals

It is only comparatively recently that there has been any such thing as a **professional** sportsperson, and only very recently that they have been paid such large amounts of money. Sometimes it is very difficult to tell the difference between a professional and an **amateur**, but there are definitions of what they should be.

• Amateurs take part in sport, or an activity, as a pastime or hobby rather than for financial gain. They take part purely for enjoyment, do not get paid and usually have a different full-time job.

• Professionals take part in a sport, or an activity, as their livelihood. They get paid for taking part and it is their full-time job.

There are also two other types of sportspeople, known as shamateurs and semi-professionals:

• **Shamateurs** are people who claim to be amateurs but are actually paid to take part. Payments they receive are illegal and unofficial under the rules of the sport in which they take part.

• **Semi-professionals** have a job, but also take part in sport, for which they are legitimately paid. Some have full-time jobs and only take part in their sport in their spare time and others have paid part-time jobs and spend the rest of their time at their sport.

Not all people who take part in sport fit neatly into any of these categories and it is often very difficult in certain sports to tell which is which. It is quite unusual to find anyone competing at the highest level in any sport who is truly an amateur because of the demands for training, practising, travelling and performing that would prevent them having a full-time job as well.

In **open sports**, such as golf, it is possible for amateurs and professionals to compete together. If there is prize money to be won, the amateurs are not usually allowed to keep it, so there may be a special award for the best-placed amateur in the competition.

An amateur football match in progress.

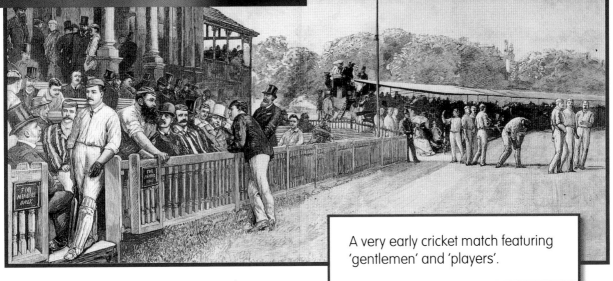

A very early cricket match featuring 'gentlemen' and 'players'.

Historical background

Before about 1900 there were very few sports with professional players, although it was quite common for wealthy people to play sport full-time. There simply was not enough money generated by sport at that time to pay people to play.

Cricket was one of the few sports with players who had the time, and independent means of income, to play. These players generally did not need to work for a living, so they were able to dedicate themselves to their chosen sport. They were called true amateurs because they received no payments or rewards for taking part, other than perhaps a trophy if they won.

Cricket's influence

In cricket there were:

- the 'gentlemen', who were wealthy and played for fun

- the 'players', who were paid to play, although it was usually only a comparatively small amount.

Most county cricket clubs could only afford one or two 'players', who were the paid professionals for the club. The rest of the team would be made up of wealthy 'gentlemen' and other amateurs.

Many sports have only become properly organized within the last 100 years or so. This has clearly had an effect on the overall growth of professional sport. The first cricket **test match** did not take place until 1877, which was the same year that the first Wimbledon tennis championship tournament was played.

The governing body of athletics is the **Amateur Athletic Association**, known as the three 'A's. It was not formed until 1880. The first football **World Cup** was not played until 1930. This has meant that many sports do not have the same tradition of professional players that cricket does.

Many sports had to first become organized, obtain sponsorship, generate media interest and build stadiums before there was enough income and money to support professionals. Even now, many sports do not have any professional players because the sport does not generate enough money to pay them.

All sports started as amateur, but the majority now have professionals who take part at the highest level, as well as amateurs who play at lower levels. Most sports have their own rules about what is allowed for a player to maintain his or her **amateur status**.

Changes towards open sport

There were professional players in tennis as long ago as 1926 but these players were not allowed to play in any of the major world events (known as the **grand slam** events). They had to play in specially arranged tournaments. This situation existed until 1968 when Wimbledon finally broke down the barriers between the amateurs and professionals and ran the first open tournament. This influenced the organizers of many other sports who could see that the barriers needed to be removed officially. Players in most of the sports had managed to find ways around the rules anyway (see page 23).

In 1988 tennis was readmitted to the Olympic Games. It was one of several sports that were allowed into the Olympic programme despite previously being considered as professional sports. In fact, the Olympic movement changed their rules to allow amateurs to receive prize money and appearance money. Professional sportspeople such as tennis players and basketball players now compete openly in the Olympics. The number of sports included in the Olympic programme increases with each Games, and more of the traditionally professional games are being admitted. When the 'Dream Team' US basketball squad (the whole squad was made up of full-time professional basketball players) was allowed to compete at the 1992 Barcelona Games, there was a great deal of controversy and media criticism. Since then this situation has been accepted more.

Another sport that had maintained very strict barriers between amateurs and professionals was rugby football. There were two forms of rugby created in 1895, when there was a dispute over professional and amateur status. Then, in 1995, the sport took on open status. The players were allowed to play both versions if they wished, and they could be paid for playing either. Up until then there had been no professional Rugby Union players allowed at all.

The growth and development of professional rugby has meant that players are now able to play all the year round. The standards of the game have improved as the players are also able to train full-time. Many players now play Rugby League for part of the season and Rugby Union for the rest. The Rugby League organizers have made their sport a summer activity instead of a winter one.

Rod Laver was the winner of the first open Wimbledon tournament.

Overcoming the rules

There were, and still are, many ways of getting around the rules that amateur sportspeople were supposed to obey. These include:

- *trust funds* – money earned through sport is paid into a fund that is not supposed to be used while the sportsperson is actually performing, but is only to be used when they 'retire'. This was a very popular method among rugby players and athletes.

- *occupations* – some of the 'jobs' that sportspeople have are specifically arranged to allow them to take part in their sport and get a wage. They are just token occupations with responsibilities that do not actually involve them in doing any proper work at all. In many countries being a member of any of the uniformed services is just such a career. Many of the former communist countries of Europe had entire teams drawn from their armies.

- *scholarships* – many universities and colleges offer sports scholarships that allow almost full-time sport to be played, with little or no actual studying required

- *expenses payments* – these are often far higher than actually needed, and effectively amount to payment for taking part

- *illegal payments* – this is often referred to as **boot money**, from the old practice of putting money in players' boots at the end of a match as a way of paying them, illegally, for performing

- *gifts* – items such as luxury cars are given as prizes or gifts, and can later be traded for cash

- *sponsorship* – all the various types of sponsorship can be used to the advantage of the performers.

A professional Rugby League player in action. Prior to 1995 Rugby League players were the only professional rugby players.

The whole issue of drug-taking by sportspeople is very controversial, and has been especially so over recent years.

Drug-taking in sport has gone on for many years, but it has increased in recent times due to:

- the highly advanced types of drugs that are now available

- the pressures and high financial rewards, that can tempt a performer to use them.

What are drugs?

A drug is a chemical substance that, when introduced into the body, can alter the biochemical system.

Most drugs are designed to improve an imbalance caused by a disease or an illness. For example, a simple and common drug is paracetamol. If you take paracetamol for a headache, the pain goes away because of the changes caused in your body. However, when drugs are used in a healthy body they do not always have the desired effect. All drugs have some sort of **side effects**.

The law and drugs

In 1971 the Misuse of Drugs Act was introduced in the UK. It identified a list of dangerous or harmful substances and called them **controlled drugs**. These fall into three categories (classes) and there are different penalties for unauthorized possession or abuse of these substances. These classes are based on the potential harmfulness of each drug. The main ones listed are:

- *Class A* – ecstasy, LSD, heroin, cocaine, crack, magic mushrooms, amphetamines (if prepared for injection)

- *Class B* – amphetamines, methylphenidate (ritalin), pholcodine

- *Class C* – cannabis, tranquillizers, some painkillers, gamma hydroxybutyrate (GHB), ketamine.

These drugs are often called **social drugs** because they are used by all sorts of people in society for a variety of reasons, but they are, nevertheless, illegal.

Drugs are taken in a variety of ways, using different methods. Some drugs are injected, using a syringe, directly into the bloodstream.

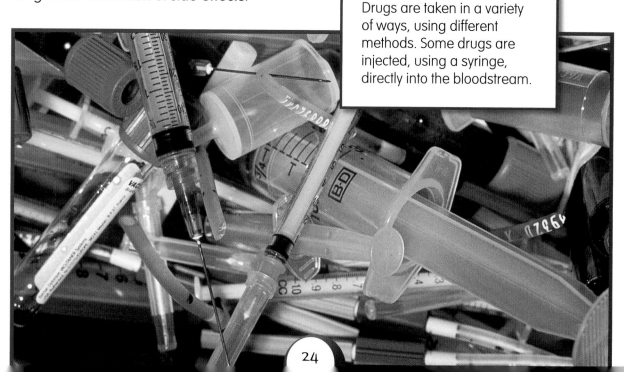

The penalties for drug conviction range from life imprisonment for dealing a Class A drug to two years imprisonment and/or unlimited fine for possession of a Class C drug.

There is evidence of sportspeople using these drugs (see pages 33–35), but there is little to indicate that their performance is improved. In many cases using these drugs is a disadvantage.However, if a player is found to be using any of the drugs listed above they will probably face police prosecution. In addition, their sport's governing body will discipline them.

Most sportspeople who are involved in drug-taking do so in the hope that it will make them perform better. These drugs are known as **performance-enhancing drugs**. They are banned by the World Anti-Doping Agency and each year the World Anti-Doping Code includes the Prohibited List that sets all of the international standards.

From 2007, the prohibited substances were listed as:
S1 – anabolic agents
S2 – hormones and related substances
S3 – **beta2agonists**
S4 – agents with anti-estrogenic activity
S5 – diuretics and other masking agents
S6 – stimulants
S7 – narcotics
S8 – cannabinoids
S9 – glucocorticosteroids.

Prohibited methods were listed as:
M1 – enhancement of oxygen transfer
M2 – chemical and physical manipulation
M3 – gene doping.

Substances prohibited in particular sports were listed as:

P1 – alcohol (eight sports are listed)
P2 – beta blockers (17 sports are listed).

Many of these drugs are not strictly illegal, although it is illegal to deal in, sell, supply or obtain anabolic **steroids**. The governing bodies of all sports have banned their use and taken steps to stop performers from using them.

The fact that using these drugs can actually improve a player's performance is what has led to their being banned. This may seem confusing when some of them, such as alcohol and beta blockers, are so easily available. These substances can be used to advantage but, more importantly, they can have damaging side effects.

National Anti-Doping Policy

UK Sport is the UK's high performance sports agency and it administers the rules relating to drugs in sport. They want drug-free sport and have pledged: 'To use the UK's role as a world leader to promote drug-free sport and help create a sporting environment in which doping is not tolerated.'

Through the National Anti-Doping Policy, UK Sport aims to:

• protect athletes and other participants in sport in the UK

• promote doping-free sport in the UK

• establish consistent standards of anti-doping policy, testing and education across the UK

• encourage and build upon national and international harmonization of anti-doping in sport.

The types and effects of some of the banned drugs are as follows.

Anabolic agents (steroids)

Anabolic agents are probably the best known and most commonly abused drugs in sport. They are certainly the ones that have been the most controversial and most discussed in the media. The main type is anabolic androgenic steroids (most commonly called steroids). These are both natural and synthetic compounds that are very similar to the male hormone **testosterone**. Testosterone has two main effects:

- androgenic – this promotes the development of male characteristics

- anabolic – this stimulates the build-up of muscle tissue.

More than 100 types of anabolic steroid are available. The most common ones are **nandrolone**, testosterone, **stanozolol**, and **boldenone**. They are usually taken in tablet form, but some of the steroids are taken by injection directly into the muscles.

Steroids were originally developed because they helped to cure anaemic conditions (a lack of iron in the body), eased wasting conditions and bone diseases, and were useful in the treatment of breast cancer.

Unfortunately, sports performers began to see some of the possible benefits from taking this type of drug. The first recorded cases of performers taking them were in the 1950s when some bodybuilders and weightlifters started to use them.

This has now spread to many other sports where the performers feel that it can help their performance by:

- increasing muscle strength

- enabling them to train harder and for longer

- increasing their competitiveness.

There is no real evidence to back up claims that these drugs can have such a marked effect, but there is evidence to suggest that they can help with training. Taking steroids can enable a performer to work harder in training sessions. Because of this they are often called **training drugs**. They are often used during the build-up to a season, competition or tournament. The performer stops taking the drug far enough in advance of the competition to make sure that no traces of it are found during pre-event testing. This can make it very difficult to detect the use of the drug, and it is the reason why many of the sport governing bodies reserve the right to drug-test their performers at any time during the year, and often during their training periods.

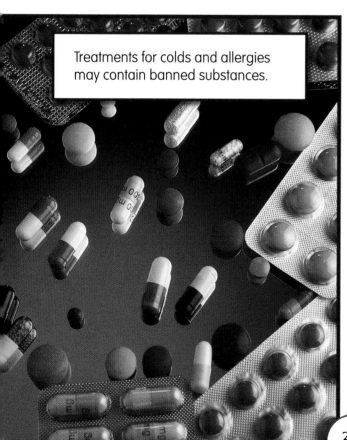

Treatments for colds and allergies may contain banned substances.

A sprinter who uses steroids as a training aid would only need a 10 per cent improvement to change from being a borderline international athlete to become a world record holder. This fact has led to several performers giving in to temptation.

Risks of steroids

The risks involved in taking steroids are quite serious, and the list of side effects is horrific.

- Liver disorders and heart disease – there can be serious damage to the liver structure, leading to jaundice, liver failure, liver tumours and bleeding in the liver. In one case a 26-year-old bodybuilder who had been using steroids for several years died of cancer of the liver as direct result of taking the drugs. The heart can be affected by changes in its fatty substance. This can lead to an increased risk of heart attacks and strokes, as well as increased blood pressure.

- Sexual and physique problems – in children, growth can be affected or even stunted. In some sports, such as gymnastics, performers start serious training while they are still children. They could be tempted to use drugs, or even encouraged to do so by adults who should know better. Men can suffer from reduced sperm production and even sterility, preventing them from fathering children. There can be shrinking of the testicles, impotence, and even the growth of breasts in men. Women can have a disruption of the menstrual cycle and ovulation, changes in the sex organs, balding, acne, growth of facial hair and deepening of the voice. In pregnant women, steroids can cause miscarriage, stillbirth or damage to the foetus – especially during early pregnancy.

- Behavioural effects – there can be quite marked changes in behaviour in some individuals. There may be increased moodiness, mood swings and aggression. The changes can be so extreme that they actually constitute a psychiatric disorder. There are several recorded instances of the wives of bodybuilders who have been taking steroids reporting that their husbands have become very aggressive and violent as a result.

How much a user is affected by these side effects and disorders depends upon the type and amount of steroids being taken and the period of time they are used. The effects can be reversed if their use is stopped soon enough. Beta2agonists are also classed as stimulants. This means they have anabolic effects, and can have similar side effects.

The side effects of corticosteroids are also quite serious. They include:

- high blood pressure

- salt and water retention

- potassium loss

- bone and muscle weakness

- mental disturbances such as euphoria (an extreme feeling of well-being or optimism), depression or paranoia (an extreme feeling of being persecuted or picked on)

- diabetes

- suppression of growth in children.

All of these side effects have been shown to exist, so it is not surprising that the authorities ban the use of these drugs to protect the performers. What is amazing is that any of the performers continue to use them, knowing just how damaging they can be.

Hormones and related substances

These drugs are based on substances that occur naturally in the body and are therefore quite difficult to detect when used illegally. Possibly for this reason, they are being used increasingly by performers. They fall into five main categories:

- chorionic gonadotrophin (HCC – Human Chorionic Gonadotrophin) has the effect of increasing the existing levels of androgenic steroids in the body and also increases levels of the male hormone testosterone

- corticotrophin (ACTH) is used to increase the levels of corticosteroids and increase the levels of euphoria that they give

- growth hormone (HGH, somatrophin) is used to increase growth and can have some very serious side effects. A disease called Creutzfeldt Jacob's disease, which affects the nervous system, can be contracted when growth hormone is obtained from impure sources. This can prove fatal.

- erythropoietin (EPO) occurs naturally in the kidneys and regulates the production of red blood cells. It can have a similar effect to **blood doping** (see page 31).

- insulin is a natural hormone that is secreted from the pancreas. Insulin is taken in injected form to control the levels of glucose in the body. It can be used in conjunction with anabolic steroids to help build muscles.

All of the above banned substances are already present in the human body, but drug

The margin between winning and losing can be a very small one and many sprinters are tempted to take performance-enhancing drugs.

misuse increases the levels artificially. If these higher levels are detected, the sportsperson can be banned.

Beta2agonists

Beta2agonists is an unusual group of stimulant drugs that are classed as being both stimulants and anabolic agents.

Agents with anti-estrogenic activity

These are substances that work to change the sensitive balance of the sex hormones in the body. They can cause serious side effects and changes in the bodies of both men and women and are now prohibited. These substances can prevent testosterone turning into feminizing hormones. This may result in higher levels of masculinizing hormones and the blocking of other necessary hormones.

Diuretics and other masking agents

Masking agents are substances that are used to prevent the detection of other substances or methods used by an athlete in doping. Used under medical supervision, these drugs reduce excess body fluids and help control high blood pressure. Sports performers could misuse them:

• to reduce weight quickly in sports where weight categories are important. (Activities such as boxing or any of the **martial arts** have particular, very strict weight categories that the competitors must fit into. Also, in some sports such as gymnastics, and horse racing it is an advantage to be lightweight.)

• to reduce the concentration of illegal/ banned substances by diluting the urine.

Because of this second effect, some authorities reserve the right to obtain urine samples from competitors at the **weigh-in** prior to a competition. A weight loss achieved

artificially, by means of these drugs, could be dangerous for the performer because it weakens the body. There are recorded examples of jockeys taking these drugs.

Stimulants

These substances increase alertness, reduce fatigue (extreme physical tiredness in the body or muscles that can prevent a performer carrying on) and may increase a user's competitiveness and hostility. They can also produce a loss of judgement and this can obviously be potentially dangerous and lead to accidents in some sports. An overdose of stimulants can even cause death. This has happened twice in cycling events – once in an Olympic event and once in the Tour de France. Other side effects can include:

• high blood pressure and headaches

• strokes and increased and irregular heartbeats

• anxiety and tremors

• insensitivity to serious injuries

• addiction.

Many of the compounds found in stimulants are also found in the treatments for colds, hay fever and asthma, so it is very important to check with a pharmacist before you take any medications before an event. Top performers always have to keep a very detailed record of any medications they are taking, so that they can disclose them during any drug-testing procedure and they can be taken into consideration later. The testing procedure is very thorough and will show up traces of any drugs that the performer has taken, even if they have taken them for a good reason.

Another recognized stimulant is caffeine, which is normally found in both tea and coffee. There is a maximum level of 12 micrograms per millilitre, above which it would be considered to be performance enhancing. Cocaine is another stimulant and it is one of the controlled, and therefore illegal, drugs.

It is fairly easy to identify sporting activities where the use of stimulants could possibly improve performance. Unfortunately, many performers have taken them in the past to help them keep going whilst competing or to work harder when they are training.

Narcotic analgesics (narcotics)

Narcotics include morphine, heroin and codeine. The main reason they are banned is because they hide the effects of illness and injury. Codeine, for instance, is found in many painkillers, some of which are freely available and can be taken in tablet form for headaches and flu symptoms. They suppress pain, but possible side effects include:

• respiratory depression

• physical and psychological dependence

• exhaustion or over training

• constipation

• extreme apathy (lack of interest in what you are doing).

Performers must be very careful to draw the line between treating an injury and actually concealing its full extent by taking narcotic analgesics. A far more serious injury might occur if the drugs are hiding the effects of something that started off as relatively minor. The body normally needs time to recover, and taking these drugs can mean that this process does not occur. The drugs will not cure the problem, and will only be a temporary way of overcoming the symptoms. Obviously, with the pressures of many competitions, performers may inevitably be tempted!

Cannabinoids

Cannabinoids basically consist of the street drugs marijuana and hashish that act as relaxants, but may also lead to a loss of coordination and concentration.

Glucocorticosteroids

Glucocorticosteroids are widely prescribed as treatments for many conditions on the skin and in the eyes, ears and nose. In addition they are used by inhalation for asthma and by local injection to treat a variety of medical conditions such as inflammation of the joints. The side effects of abuse can be weakness of bones, impaired tissue repair and reduced immune functions with increased susceptibility to infection.

Beta blockers

Beta blockers are prescribed to people who have a medical condition affecting their heart. These drugs calm and control the heart rate.

Use of beta blockers is banned in shooting events.

In some activities they would not be of any real benefit, but in others they have been identified as advantageous, since they can have a calming effect, for example stopping any minor shakes when the player is shooting or concentrating. Beta blockers are therefore banned in:

- archery
- shooting
- modern pentathlon (shooting events are included here)
- diving and synchronized swimming
- bobsleigh
- luge (a form of bobsleigh)
- ski jumping
- freestyle skiing
- snooker.

The use of beta blockers in events requiring endurance would actually harm the player's performance, but there have been cases where they have been used in sports to calm nerves and keep the performer steady.

Enhancement of oxygen transfer

Some years ago, endurance athletes used a blood doping technique to make their blood more efficient in carrying and supplying oxygen. In blood doping, extra blood is added into the bloodstream. This blood may have been taken from the same athlete previously, forcing the remaining blood to produce extra red blood cells to replace those lost. When the blood is added back into the bloodstream, there is an increased number of red blood cells that can carry extra oxygen around the body. As oxygen is one of the main sources of energy used over an

extended period of time by any athlete taking part in long-distance endurance events, this clearly gives an unfair advantage. Although it is more common to use the athlete's own blood, it can also be done with someone else's blood, red blood cells or related products. Any method of artificially enhancing the uptake, transport or delivery of oxygen is also banned.

Blood doping used to be tolerated, and some athletes openly admitted that it was something that they did, but it is now banned. Possible side effects include:

- development of allergic reactions such as a rash or fever
- acute kidney damage if the incorrect blood type is used
- delayed transfusion reaction, which can result in a fever and jaundice
- transmission of infectious diseases such as viruses, hepatitis and AIDS
- overload of the circulation and metabolic shock.

Doping control

The use of drugs to improve performance is clearly cheating. It can also be harmful, sometimes even fatal. Some performers use a variety of drugs from the different categories in an attempt to improve their performance, despite all the warnings and evidence of the harm it is doing them. There is a procedure in place to try to catch those who do use drugs, and to discourage others from starting to do so. The procedure is called **doping control** and it involves obtaining a urine sample, testing it for any banned substances and following that up with any disciplinary procedures that might be necessary.

Chemical and physical manipulation

Tampering, or attempting to tamper, with samples in order to alter the integrity and validity of samples collected in doping controls, is also banned. This can include intravenous transfusions, catheterisation and urine substitution.

Gene doping

The use of cells, genes, genetic elements or changing the way genes can affect the way the body works, in order to enhance athletic performance, is also prohibited. Gene doping is also tested for through doping control.

How doping control works

The testing procedure is as follows and it is the step-by-step process that all performers must go through if they are tested for drugs:

1. Notifying the athlete

Competitors can be chosen for testing either in or out of competition and will then be notified that they have been selected for testing. They will be allowed to finish their training before they report to the Doping Control Station at a stated time. In many competitions they will be asked to report immediately after the sporting event has taken place.

2. Reporting for testing

The competitor may be accompanied to the Doping Control Station where sealed, non-alcoholic drinks are available and a representative from the sports governing body might also be present.

3. Selecting a collection vessel

The competitor chooses the container for the urine sample from the selection available. These containers are all numbered.

4. Providing a sample under supervision

The competitor removes enough clothing to satisfy the Independent Sampling Officer (**ISO**), who must be able to observe the sample being given. Only the competitor handles the sample and then returns to the administration room.

5. Selecting the sample containers

The competitor is allowed to select two containers between which the urine sample will be divided.

6. Breaking the security seals

The competitor breaks the security seals on the bottles or containers.

7. Dividing the sample

The sample is divided between the two sample bottles or containers.

8. Sealing the samples

The ISO checks the container seals and then the competitor seals them up. He or she then labels the containers: A and B.

9. Recording the information

The container code numbers and seal numbers are filled in and checked by the competitor, who may then declare any medications that they have taken the previous week.

10. Certifying the information

The ISO, the competitor and the competitor's representative (if present) then sign a form if they are satisfied with the procedure. A copy of the Doping Control Collection Form is given to the competitor who is then free to go.

11. Transferring the samples to the laboratory

Both the samples are sent by a secure system to an accredited laboratory for analysis. Only the sample, seal and medication information is forwarded. The competitor's name, or any other information, is not included.

12. Reporting the result

The report on the A sample is usually available within 10 days. If the result is negative, the governing body is informed and the B sample is destroyed. Results can be given within 24 hours if a major competition is in progress. This is certainly the case in the Olympics where the first three athletes in all events are routinely tested.

If the result is positive the following procedure starts.

- The competitor may be suspended from competition and the second (B) sample can be analysed. The competitor is also allowed to present their case.

- A decision is made on the punishment to be given. This can range from suspension for a given period of time, to a lifetime ban.

- Every competitor is allowed to appeal against the decisions.

The testing procedure is thought to be as fair as possible. If a competitor refuses to be tested, it is considered to be the same as providing a positive sample and punishments will be set.

Recommended sanctions

Sanctions (punishments) now tend to vary greatly between sports and also between the governing bodies that have responsibility for dealing with their own performers according to their own particular codes of practice.

Drug abuse in sport

The first recorded use of drugs dates from 1865. There are many other recorded cases where performers have used drugs to improve their performance. Some important landmarks in drug testing are listed below:

- 1955 – 25 urine tests were carried out on cyclists in a race in France and 5 proved positive.

- 1962 – The **IOC** (International Olympic Committee) passed a resolution against doping.

- 1968 – Drug testing was introduced to the Winter and Summer Olympics. Interestingly, not one sample proved positive. This started a debate over whether the sport was 'clean', or that the testing was outdated and inadequate and was simply not catching the guilty people.

- 1976 – The first tests for steroids were used.

- 1988 – In the Seoul Olympics there were 10 positive doping results. Five of these results were in weightlifting, two in the modern pentathlon, one each in wrestling and judo, and one in athletics. The athlete found guilty was Canadian sprinter Ben Johnson. This became one of the most famous drugs cases because Johnson had just won the Olympic 100-metres title. He was banned for two years and returned to racing with little success. He later failed another test and was banned for life from the sport.

- 1999 – The World Anti-Doping Agency was formed. In 2004 it published the World Anti-Doping Code, to be standardized across all sports.

There is little in sport more controversial than the drug situation and many athletes have battled against the authorities after being banned.

- **1989** – Trine Hattestad, the women's European javelin champion, was given a two-year ban for taking steroids. The ban was set aside and she was awarded US$50,000 compensation when it was decided that the amount of steroid found was too small to be significant.

- **1990** – The US world 400-metre champion, Butch Reynolds, was found guilty of taking steroids and claimed mistaken identity. He took his appeal all the way to the US Supreme Court but still had to serve a two-year suspension. He returned to competition after the ban and continued to protest his innocence, but had probably missed out on potentially his most successful period as an athlete due to the ban.

- **1991** – The German world 100-metre and 200-metre champion Katrin Krabbe successfully appealed against manipulation of a test in 1991 on a legal technicality. She also escaped on a technicality in 1992 after traces of the beta2agonist clenbuturol were found, but was eventually banned for bringing the sport into disrepute.

- **1994** – Diane Modahl, a British middle distance runner, was tested positive for traces of testosterone. She appealed against the test, which had shown her to have 42 times the normal amount. There was great controversy about how her sample had been stored at the testing laboratory. It was not until 1995 that she was eventually cleared. She returned to athletics but was unable to achieve her previous best due to the time she had been forced out of competition.

British sprinter Dwain Chambers (right) has seen his career damaged by a ban for taking prohibited substances. Shortly after his return to competitive racing he was part of the winning 4 x 100 metres relay team at the European Championships in Sweden in 2006, but was shunned by teammate Darren Campbell (left) during victory celebrations.

China

China as a nation had not taken part in international competition for many years, but when its competitors returned in the early 1990s there was much suspicion about the standards they managed to achieve. Their runners and swimmers, in particular, dominated in many events despite not having competed outside their own country previously. After many complaints from other countries the Chinese began to drug-test their performers.

Following the World Swimming Championships in 1994, seven Chinese swimmers tested positive for drug use. All had been using a form of the male hormone testosterone, which acted as a steroid. This brief period of sporting dominance stopped almost as soon as regular drug testing was started, and the suspicions of other countries seemed to be justified. Chinese athletes are once again making a greater impression in international competitions. With the 2008 Olympics being held in the Chinese capital, Beijing, there is worldwide interest in the performance of the country's sportspeople.

More recent cases

The Tour de France cycle race has been dogged by drug scandals for many years. In 1998 there was a doping scandal in which French officials caught an employee of the Festina cycling team with performance-enhancing drugs, including erythropoietin (EPO). Following various arrests linked to the case, six of Festina's nine riders – including team leader Christophe Moreau – conceded that they had used performance-enhancing drugs. Later that year Moreau tested positive for anabolic steroids.

In 2002 Stefano Garzelli, the leader of the VINI Caldirola team, tested positive for a diuretic drug and Igor Gonzalez de Galdeano was banned for having excessive levels of an anti-asthma drug. In 2004 French police seized male hormones, EPO and amphetamines, and arrested two cyclists, following an anti-doping investigation involving Cofidas, one of France's top teams and home to three world champions. In 2006, the winner of that year's Tour de France, American Floyd Landis, failed a drugs test related to testosterone levels.

In 2005, after a long investigation, the founders of BALCO, a US company, pleaded guilty to distributing steroids and financial crimes. BALCO's activities led to accusations against many people from a range of sports, including athletes Dwain Chambers, Marion Jones and Tim Montgomery, as well as baseball and American football players.

In 2006 cricket saw the banning of the two Pakistan fast bowlers Shoaib Akhtar and Mohammed Asif for failing a drugs test. Both players were reported to have tested positive for nandrolone (a banned steroid). Shoaib was banned for two years and Asif banned for one, though their punishments were overturned on appeal.

There has been an increasing amount of out-of-competition testing in many sports. In 2006, Greek athletes Kostas Kenteris and Katerina Thanou accepted that they had broken anti-doping test rules before the 2004 Athens Olympic Games, from which they had surprisingly withdrawn. The UK's athletes too are subject to a very rigorous system, which requires them to notify authorities of their whereabouts at all times, so they can be tested at any time. In 2006, Britain's World Triathlon champion Tim Don was banned for three months for missing three out-of-competition tests.

5 Politics and sport

It is almost impossible to keep politics out of sport. Sport in most countries is financed, or at least monitored, from government level and is therefore interrelated with politics.

The UK has a minister responsible for sport who is very influential and can advise the various sporting bodies. In some countries, especially the former communist countries, sport was a political priority area. The state was in complete control of it. The degree of control in the old communist countries was shown when they **boycotted** some of the Olympic Games (for example, in 1980) and refused to send their athletes. Their political systems meant that they could do this. In a similar situation the UK could only advise their athletes against going and could not actually stop them from taking part.

Politics helping sport

It is often thought that politicians only influence sport in a negative way, but this is not strictly true. In the UK, without government backing there would be far less provision of facilities and funding. Past and present governments have also ensured that sport is, by law, part of the range of educational subjects that must be taught in schools, within a varied physical education programme.

Another positive move has been the setting up of various sports bodies such as the Sports Council, and the provision of extra funds from such sources as the National Lottery. If there are any major problems associated with sport then the Government will act.

The Taylor enquiry, which followed the Heysall Stadium and Hillsborough disasters, was set up to find solutions to problems of controlling large crowds in stadiums. The results of this enquiry were welcomed and money was made available for improvements that benefited all types of sport.

There is no doubt that in many communist countries the political systems raised the standards of sport. Sport was given a very high profile. Most athletes and sportspeople in those countries did not consider that their government was interfering with sport, but were more likely to think it was giving them valuable assistance. However, we now know that the communist system also led to many abuses of its athletes, including widespread use of drugs to boost performance.

Politicians have helped increase safety and control at stadiums.

The Berlin Wall was pulled down in 1992. This helped Germany's national sports teams as East and West could now work together.

The collapse of the former communist bloc in 1990 was a major turning point in the way sport was organized there. The old ways of running sport – under tight government control – changed drastically. However, the loss of the large amounts of money that had previously been spent on sport led to a fall in standards in many of these countries.

Political issues

The relationship between politics and sport has not always been easy, and has often been very controversial. There have been many occasions when politics has interfered with sport. Some are listed here:

- **1908** – Finland's Olympic team had to parade without its flag because Russia, which ruled Finland at that time, would not allow it. The US team did not like decisions made by the all-British appeal jury and staged a demonstration in New York.

- **1912** – There were more protests by Russia that Finland should not have its own flag, and the Austro-Hungarian Empire protested that Bohemia and Hungary should not be allowed to compete separately.

There was also a very strong rumour, which was never proved, that the African-American sprinter Howard Drew was withdrawn from the 100-metres final so that the winner would not be a black athlete. The official reason given for his withdrawal was that he had injured a tendon. Swedish newspapers claimed that he was locked in the changing rooms by his own officials during the final!

- **1920** – The Olympic Games were held in Antwerp, Belgium, immediately after World War I. Germany and its wartime allies were not sent an invitation to take part.

- **1925** – The year following the Paris Olympics, the Soviet Union's Communist Party made a declaration that 'sport should be used as a means of rallying the broad masses of workers and peasants around the various Party and trade union organizations through which the masses of workers and peasants are to be drawn into social and political activity'. This set the tone for the communist attitude towards sport for the next 65 years and made it an obvious political tool.

The Berlin Olympics of 1936 was dominated by Hitler's influence.

- **1936** – The Olympics were held in Berlin, Germany. In 1933, Adolph Hitler's Nazi Party had come to power. Hitler decided to use the games as a massive **propaganda exercise** (a way of sending out misleading and biased information). He believed that there was a master race in Germany known as the Aryans and that Jews and other races and religions were to be despised and persecuted. Many of the other countries' teams considered boycotting the Games. The decision to hold the Games in Berlin had been made in 1931, when the political situation had not been foreseen.

The Games were really dominated by one man: Jesse Owens, the African-American athlete, who won four gold medals. His success, along with other African-Americans in the US team, was a great embarrassment to Hitler and undermined plans to prove the supremacy of Aryans.

- **1940** – There were no Olympic Games held, and very few other sporting contests either, as most major countries were fighting World War II. Although some sport carried on at a local level, it was impossible to have properly organized international sport.

- **1948** – South Africa introduced the **apartheid** laws, which enforced a policy of racial segregation within that country. This meant that black and non-white people were denied rights, as well as facilities and opportunities. They were not considered for any of the national teams in any sporting areas and had to lead separate lives from the white population. This led to a great deal of criticism from other countries throughout the world. It became a major political issue, causing many problems in South Africa's relationships with other countries for years afterwards.

- **1949** – A New Zealand rugby team was banned from touring South Africa because the team contained Maori players, who would not be considered acceptable under the apartheid laws introduced there.

- **1954** – China was finally admitted to the Olympics, despite not accepting the **IOC** decision to recognize its neighbour state of Taiwan, which China still refused to acknowledge.

- **1954** – China withdrew from the Olympic movement (over the dispute about Taiwan) and started a boycott of sports organizations and competitions.

- **1964** – South Africa was banned from the Olympic movement because of the apartheid laws. This led to a long period of demonstrations and boycotts throughout the world. The South Africans even arranged **rebel tours** where they paid foreign sport stars to come and play against them (mainly rugby and cricket players). The performers who took part were often subsequently banned in their own countries as a result.

- **1970** – A state of war was declared between Honduras and El Salvador after a World Cup qualifying game. Also the South African cricket team was asked not to tour England after a formal request from the British Home Secretary, James Callaghan.

- **1976** – Some African countries boycotted the Montréal Olympics in protest at a New Zealand rugby team touring South Africa.

- **1980** – The United States and 51 other nations boycotted the Moscow Olympics as a protest against the Soviet Union's invasion of Afghanistan.

- **1984** – The Soviet Union and 14 other nations boycotted the Los Angeles Olympics, mainly as retaliation for the action taken in 1980, but officially for security reasons and as a protest over the commercialization of the Games.

- **1990** – The communist system in Eastern Europe began to crumble after political change. Many smaller nations became independent and joined in world sport.

- **1992** – South Africa finally abolished the apartheid system and was readmitted to world sport and the Barcelona Olympic Games where they fielded a mixed team.

- **2001** – The Irish Gaelic Athletic Association (GAA) lifted a ban on members of the Royal Ulster Constabulary and British army from playing Gaelic games. This was as a result of the improved political situation in Northern Ireland. (In 2005, the GAA also voted to allow 'foreign games' to be played in its stadiums, such as Croke Park.)

- **2001** – Several international sports events were moved away from Pakistan and the rest of the Indian subcontinent. This was because of fears about security after the terrorist attacks on the World Trade Center towers and the Pentagon building in the USA on 11 September.

- **2004** – The political tensions in Zimbabwe resulted in Australian cricketer Stuart McGill making himself unavailable for a tour there because of what he described as gross human rights abuses. A one-day international between England and Zimbabwe was postponed following the Zimbabwe government's banning of 13 British **journalists** from the country. The previous year the England team had pulled out of a **World Cup** one-day match in Zimbabwe citing security concerns.

- **2006** – Following a two-year power struggle over control of Nigerian football, a new chairman of the country's football association was finally elected following a dispute between the Nigerian government and **FIFA**. The Nigerian government claimed that as it funded most of the country's sports activities it could dictate how the football should be run. FIFA disagreed and its pressure forced an election to be held.

- **2006** – The president of Iran confirmed that he had ordered the Ministry of Sport to give permission to allow women to attend World Cup football games, without coverir their heads and bodies in line with Islamic dress codes. This effectively removed the ban on women in the football stadiums that had come into force in 1979 with the Islamic revolution in Iran. The old ruling had in effect stopped women from attending matches.

After a ban of almost 30 years, South Africa were readmitted to the Olympics in 1992. Here in Barcelona the South African team was not all-white, but consisted of sportspeople from many different races.

Technological change and sport

Throughout the history of sport there has been continual – if gradual – change and improvement. However, the developments have been far more rapid in recent years. The major changes have been in equipment and materials.

Equipment

Equipment for players

The equipment available today for people taking part in sport is far more varied, safer, and better designed than it has ever been before. It is also constantly changing – so much so that governing bodies have to keep checks to ensure that it is legal and does not give anyone an unfair advantage. The impact these changes have made can be seen in these particular sports:

- *Racket sports* – it is only over the last 20 years or so that wooden rackets have been replaced by ones made of aluminium, then graphite. Using these new, lighter materials has enabled the head, and therefore the ball-striking area, to be enlarged without changing the overall length of the racket. Rackets for tennis, squash and badminton are all made from these newer materials.

There is no longer any need for racket presses, which protected the rackets and stopped them from warping, as the new materials are lighter, stronger and more stable. It is not only the rackets themselves that have new materials. Synthetic materials are also used to string the rackets, and these can give extra power to the performers.

Tennis rackets have changed greatly over the years. Wooden ones have been replaced by lighter, stronger ones, such as the one used here by Scotland's Andrew Murray during a match in France.

Dangerous javelins

The javelin has undergone many changes as more advanced materials have been used in its construction. However, they became so efficient that they became dangerous. Competitors were throwing them so far that the stadiums were not big enough. Therefore they are now reduced in weight and the position of the centre of gravity has been moved, to reduce the distances they can be thrown. This was an example of technology being too effective!

- *Athletics* – field events have benefited from improved equipment in several ways. In the modern pole vault, the pole is constructed from a lightweight fibreglass compound that makes it lighter, stronger and more flexible than the older versions. This means that the vaulters can jump much higher. For increased safety, large air-filled and purpose-built landing areas have been designed that are more suitable and efficient for use with modern equipment. They can allow a jumper to land safely after coming down from a height of nearly 7 metres. Previously the jumpers would have landed in a sandpit! The high jump also has a similar landing area that enables the jumpers to use the technique of the **Fosbury flop** (named after the first person to perform it – Richard Fosbury), without fear of harming themselves when they land on their backs.

Footwear has also undergone significant change and, in athletics, specialist shoes are now available for any of the events. With the changes and advances in the running surfaces, this is essential for an athlete. Where winning margins are so close, they must make sure that they have the most modern equipment available.

- *Cricket* – there is now a full range of protective equipment available for cricket players. Although the basic leg guard pads have not changed significantly there is now a full range of protective equipment for the head and the materials used for the other protective items are lighter and less bulky than they were. This means that the player is protected, but does not lose any mobility.

Most sporting footwear is now very specialized and specific to the sport.

Equipment for administration

As well as changes in equipment for the performer there have also been advances in technology that can help to make the sport fair, and life easier for those who are officiating. They include:

- *Accurate timing* – in events where it is essential that the timing is completely accurate, the possibility of human error has been reduced by the introduction of sophisticated machines. Electronic sensors in sprinters' starting blocks start the timing as soon as the performers leave the blocks. They are so sensitive that they can even detect a false start. They are linked to the starting gun and can register the athletes' reaction times. Other sensors register the runners as they cross the line and there is an instant read-out of the measured time, which can be displayed on TV monitor screens. A championship can be decided by one-thousandth of a second and it is only these very accurate timing devices that can separate some of the runners.

  In tennis, similar devices are used to check whether the ball is in or out of play, especially on the lines, as the ball is often travelling too fast for the human eye to judge accurately.

- *Accurate officiating* – many sports are using the advanced technology of television to help the officials. One of the first sports to do this was American football. At every game, there is a booth where extra officials check replayed action to decide whether or not the officials in the game have made correct decisions. This spread to cricket where the **third umpire** is now very common in international games. The umpires on the pitch can ask for a decision to be made for them after the extra umpire watches the TV action replayed. This technique is also used in football. The first TV-assisted match was played in Paris in April 1997. There were 24 cameras to watch the play, and headphones and microphones were used to allow the referee and fourth official to keep in contact. Electronic wristbands worn by the players tracked them for offside decisions, and microchips in the ball even showed whether it was in or out of play!

This cycling competitor at the Atlanta Olympics is wearing a heart-rate monitor. Improved technology means that sportspeople can monitor their individual fitness during training or events.

Artificial playing surfaces can be laid just about anywhere.

• *Monitoring performances* – players can be helped to monitor their own performance as they compete. It is now very common for cyclists taking part in long-distance events to have chest harnesses that constantly monitor their heart rates. These are linked up to monitors either on the handlebars or their wrists. The system enables them to work at their highest capacity and can also warn them if they are working at too high a level.

Materials

There is a wide choice of synthetic materials now available for use in sport. They range from the light, aerodynamic materials used for clothing for swimmers, speed skaters and cyclists, right through to the variety of artificial surfaces used for tennis, hockey, football, athletics and in sports halls. Previously it was only possible to use natural materials such as wood, metal, cotton, wool and leather for clothing and equipment.

The development of improved materials for playing surfaces has greatly changed the nature of some of the games. Top-class hockey is now played almost exclusively on artificial surfaces and very rarely on grass. This allows the players to benefit far more from high levels of skill, as the ball does not move about as much as it would on a bumpy grass pitch.

Artificial strips for cricket are becoming more and more popular and artificial surfaces for tennis can now be laid down almost anywhere to enable tennis tournaments and matches to be played.

Not all sports have totally endorsed these new surfaces. Both football and American football authorities initially allowed artificial surfaces to be used for their sports, but have now moved away from them. The **FA** actually banned their use, although at one time there were several league sides that used them. Now there are none in use for matches. American football teams found that they were getting a lot of injuries due to hard surfaces and many of the teams are now reverting to grass pitches – although this is obviously not possible for those with indoor stadiums!

Many facilities are benefiting from improved materials used in their construction. Gymnastic areas are now usually purpose-built with sunken areas filled with protective materials. Indoor tennis halls are far more common. Weight training and lifting equipment is now purpose-built and designed, often with in-built computers that can assist the performers in their training.

Training aids

Improved technology has led to many developments in training aids. Computers can now be used in a variety of ways, ranging from monitoring performance to simulating events. Many Formula One Grand Prix drivers actually use computerized driving simulators to 'test drive' racing circuits before they actually go there.

Watches are available that can monitor anything from training zones to heart rates and blood pressure, all of which can be done while the performer is working. Computerized machines can be used to check training levels very accurately and there is little doubt that technology is continuing to advance at a very rapid rate, giving more and more help to the committed sports performer.

Nike and iPod have combined forces to produce a new sensor. The sensor fits inside training shoes and is linked to an iPod. It can set targets for training, select different types of workout, choose music to accompany it, monitor progress, give spoken feedback, record weight and units of distance, and even link to a central database to track progress and compare results with other users!

Landing areas made from synthetic materials have increased safety levels in gyms. This is especially important for sports such as gymnastics where training starts at an early age.

Glossary

amateur someone who takes part in sport, or an activity, as a pastime or hobby, rather than for money. They take part for enjoyment only, do not get paid and usually have a different full-time job.

Amateur Athletic Association governing body of athletics

amateur status classification laid down by the rules of the sport, which dictate whether a player is an amateur or not

apartheid legal system introduced in South Africa in 1948 that discriminated against black and coloured races and segregated them from the white population, leaving them with almost no rights or opportunities

autobiography book written by a person, about their own true-life story

beta2agonists stimulant drugs

blood doping transfusion of blood to help a performance by increasing the number of oxygen-carrying red blood cells in the system

boldenone an anabolic steroid

boot money one of the names given for illegal payments made to amateurs

boycott refuse to attend an event, as a method of protest

Ceefax teletext system operated by the BBC

controlled drugs group of illegal and banned drugs

doping control system that is used by sports officials when carrying out drug testing on sports performers

FA Football Association: the ruling body of football in the UK

FIFA international body that administers world football. The letters stand for *Federation Internationale de Football Associations*.

Fosbury flop technique used in high jump, named after its founder

grand slam major events in the tennis championships throughout the world. Also used to describe major events in golf and Rugby Union.

harpaston ancient Greek game from which football and American football may have developed

hat trick expression first used in cricket if a bowler got three wickets in succession, now used in many sports for 'three in a row' achievements

hurling Irish game similar to hockey

IOC International Olympic Committee: the governing body in charge of the Olympic Games

ISO Independent Sampling Officer, present at drug testing of sports performers

journalist someone who makes a living by finding out about events or people and writing articles for newspapers or magazines

lawn tennis full name for the game of tennis that developed from real tennis

listed events protected sporting events that, by government legislation, have to be shown on terrestrial television

locker room interviews arrangement whereby players are interviewed immediately after sporting events, often in the changing area

martial arts combat sports or methods of self defence, usually of oriental origin

MCC Marylebone Cricket Club: the ruling body of cricket

monopoly situation where one person or organization has control of a market, so there is little competition

nandrolone compound with tissue-building function

NFL National Football League: the governing body of American football

open sport events or competitions that are open to both amateurs and professionals to play in together

pay per view certain sporting events that can only be seen on satellite networks if the viewer pays an extra fee

performance-enhancing drugs drugs taken by sportspeople to improve their performance

press conference meeting at which information is given to journalists

professional someone who takes part in sport, or an activity, as a means of earning their livelihood; they get paid for taking part in sport and do this as a full-time job

propaganda exercise event where misleading and biased information is given out for political purposes

real tennis form of tennis first played in the Middle Ages

rebel tours sporting tours arranged by the South African authorities who invited leading sports performers to their country, even though they were banned by the sports ruling bodies

semi-professional someone who has a job and also takes part in sport, for which they are legally paid

shamateur person who claims to be an amateur but is in fact being paid to take part, usually with illegal payments

shinty Irish game similar to hockey

side effects unwanted, and often harmful, effects that drugs can have on the user

social drugs drugs taken by people for social reasons, for pleasure or exhilaration

sphairistike ancient Greek game similar to tennis

stanozolol an anabolic agent

steroids chemical compounds similar to the male hormone, testosterone

Super Bowl climax of the American football season when the two most successful teams meet in the final game

teletext information, broadcast as printed text on television

terrestrial television television stations that can be broadcast to all homes without using a satellite

test match name given to an international match, usually in rugby or cricket

testosterone hormone that produces male characteristics

third umpire extra official in cricket who makes decisions after watching television replays

training drugs performance-enhancing drugs that allow the performer to train longer and harder

weigh-in being weighed before or after competitive sports in which weight is a qualifying factor, for example in boxing

World Cup name for the international championship, usually the football World Cup. There are now World Cup competitions in other sports, too, such as cricket.

Find out more

Books

Just the Facts: Drugs and Sport, Clive Gifford (Heinemann Library, 2004)
Making Healthy Food Choices: Food for Sports, Neil Morris (Heinemann Library, 2006)
Teen Issues: Fitness, Joanna Watson and Joanna Kedge (Raintree, 2005)
What's the Deal?: Steroids, Karla Fitzhugh (Heinemann Library, 2005)

Websites

British Olympic Association: www.olympics.org.uk
FIFA: www.fifa.com
Football Association: www.thefa.com
National Coaching Foundation: wwwncf.org.uk
National [American] Football League: www.nfl.com
Sport England: www.sportengland.org
Sports Coach: www.sportscoachuk.org
UK Sport: www.uksport.gov.uk

Index

advertising 14
Amateur Athletic Association 21
amateurs 10, 19, 20, 21, 22, 23
American football 11, 35, 43, 45
amphitheatres 4
anabolic agents 25, 26–7
apartheid 39, 40
athletics 6, 8, 35, 42
autobiographies 19

badminton 41
BALCO 35
baseball 8–9
basketball 8, 22
beta2agonists 25, 27, 29, 34
beta blockers 25, 30–1
blood doping 25, 28, 31
bodybuilding 26, 27
boot money 23
boxing 4, 8, 17, 29
boycotts 36, 40
bull dances 4–5

caffeine 30
Chambers, Dwain 34, 35
China 35, 39
chorionic gonadotrophin 28
codeine 30
combat sports 4
Commonwealth Games 12, 13
communist countries 23, 36, 37, 39
corticosteroids 25, 27, 28, 30
corticotrophin 28
Creutzfeldt Jacob's disease 28
cricket 7, 9, 12, 13, 16, 17, 21, 35,
    39, 42
cycling 33, 35, 43, 44

Derby, the 12
discus 8
diuretics 25, 29
Don, Tim 35
doping control 31–3, 35
drugs 24–35

equipment 41–4
erythropoietin (EPO) 28, 35
expenses payments 23

football 7, 10, 12, 13, 16, 17, 21, 36, 43,
    44, 45
footwear 42
Formula One 14, 17, 45

golf 20
governing bodies 8, 15, 25, 32, 33, 41
Grand National 12
Grand Prix 14, 45

grand slam events 22
Greece (ancient) 6, 7, 11
growth hormones 28
gymnastics 4, 15, 27, 45

hammer 8
Hattestad, Trine 34
hat tricks 9
high jump 8
Hitler, Adolf 38
hockey 11, 16, 44
horse racing 5, 12
horses 5
hurling 11

illegal payments 23

javelin 8, 42
jockeys 29
Johnson, Ben 33
journalists 19, 39
judo 5, 33

Krabbe, Katrin 34

listed events 12–13
locker room interviews 18
long jump 8

marathon 6–7, 33
martial arts 4, 5, 29
materials 44–45
media 12–19
minority sports 15
Modahl, Diane 34

narcotics 25, 30
National Anti-Doping Policy 25
netball 8, 16
newspapers 12, 18

officiating 43
Olympian Games 6
Olympic Games 6, 7, 12, 15, 22, 33,
    36, 37, 38, 39, 40
open sports 20, 22
organized sport, development of 6–8
origins of sports 4–11
Owens, Jesse 38

pay per view events 12, 14, 17
performance-enhancing drugs 25,
    28, 35
performances, monitoring 44
playing surfaces 44–5
pole vault 8, 42
politics 36–40
press, the 18–19

press conferences 18
prize money 20, 22
professionals 20, 21, 22
protective equipment 42

racket sports 41
radio 17
rebel tours 39
regulation of sport 8
revenue (income) 15, 16
Reynolds, Butch 34
rugby 10, 16, 22, 23, 39

satellite and cable services 13–14
scholarships 23
semi-professionals 20
shamateurs 20
shinty 11
shot-put 8
showjumping 5
social drugs 24
South Africa 38, 39, 40
sponsorship 14, 15, 21, 23
sporting contests, earliest 4–5
sports magazines 18–19
squash 11, 41
stadiums 4, 21, 36, 45
steroids 25, 26–27, 33, 34, 35
stimulants 25, 27, 29–30
Super Bowl 11

table tennis 11
television 12–17
tennis 10–11, 12, 21, 22, 41, 43, 44, 45
terrestrial television 12, 13
test matches 9, 12, 21
testosterone 26, 28, 29, 34, 35
timing devices 43, 44
Tour de France 29, 35
track and field events 8
training aids 45
training drugs 26
triple jump 8
trust funds 23

umpires 43

weight categories 29
weightlifting 26, 33, 34, 45
Wimbledon 11, 12, 21, 22
World Anti-Doping Agency 33
World Anti-Doping Code 33
World Cups 10, 12, 13, 21, 36, 39
wrestling 4, 5, 33

Zimbabwe 39